Mortimer's Math

Sorting

Karen Bryant-Mole

Gareth Stevens Publishing
MILWAUKEE

Mortimer's Math

For a free color catalog describing Gareth Stevens' list of high-quality books and multimedia programs, call 1-800-542-2595 (USA) or 1-800-461-9120 (Canada). Gareth Stevens Publishing's Fax: (414) 225-0377.

Library of Congress Cataloging-in-Publication Data available upon request from publisher. Fax: (414) 225-0377 for the attention of the Publishing Records Department.

ISBN 0-8368-2621-3

This North American edition first published in 2000 by
Gareth Stevens Publishing
1555 North RiverCenter Drive, Suite 201
Milwaukee, WI 53212 USA

This edition © 2000 by Gareth Stevens, Inc. Original © BryantMole Books, 1999. First published in 1999 by Evans Brothers Limited, 2A Portman Mansions, Chiltern Street, London W1M 1LE, United Kingdom. Additional end matter © 2000 by Gareth Stevens, Inc.

Created by Karen Bryant-Mole
Photographs by Zul Mukhida
Designed by Jean Wheeler
Teddy bear by Merrythought Ltd.

Printed in the United States of America

1 2 3 4 5 6 7 8 9 04 03 02 01 00

contents

sorting

Mortimer the bear is picking up his toys.
He is putting the animals into the red basket,
the cars into the yellow basket,
and the food into the blue basket.

I am making
a group of animals,
a group of cars, and
a group of food.

Putting things into groups is called sorting.
Help Mortimer finish sorting his toys.
Tell him where each toy belongs.

sets

Mortimer loves drawing and painting.

I have a group of felt pens, a group of pencils, and a group of paintbrushes.

A group of objects
that belong together
is called a set.

a set of colored pencils

a set of
paintbrushes

a set of felt pens

color

Mortimer is sorting his clothespins
into sets of different colors.

I am making a green set, a red set, and a blue set.

Mortimer still has some clothespins to sort. To which pile does each belong?

shape

Mortimer's blocks are different shapes.

I am sorting my blocks by shape.

Here are some buttons
that have been sorted
by shape.

a set of triangles

a set of circles

a set of squares

material

Mortimer's boat is made of plastic.
His car is made of metal.

Plastic and metal are different kinds of materials.

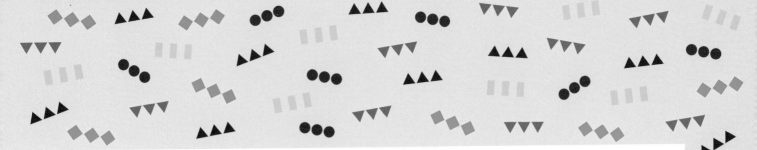

These things have been sorted by material.

a set of plastic objects

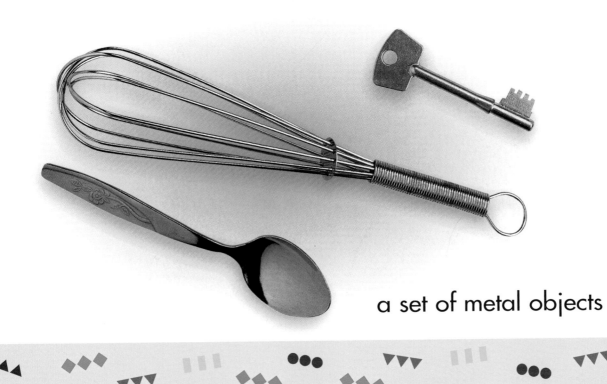

a set of metal objects

texture

Mortimer is ready for a bath.

My towel feels soft. The soap and the soap dish feel hard.

The way something feels is called its texture.

Here are some more objects that
have been sorted by texture.

a set of soft objects

a set of hard objects

at home

You can sort things
any way you choose.

All these
things belong in
my bedroom.

Some of these objects are used in the garden, some are used in the kitchen, and some are used in the bathroom.

Which things belong together?

in the garden

in the kitchen

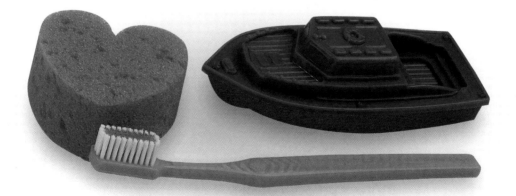

in the bathroom

different sets

Mortimer is getting ready to drink tea.

I can sort my dishes in more than one way.

Look at everything very carefully.
Can you think of two different
ways to sort the dishes?

I can also sort my dishes by color.

Find some of your own toys and see how many different ways you can sort them.

glossary/index

group — a collection of things or people gathered together 5, 6, 7

material — what something is made of, such as metal, plastic, cloth, or wood 12-13

metal — a material, such as gold or silver, that is usually shiny and hard 12, 13

plastic — a strong yet lightweight material made from chemicals in factories 12, 13

set — a group of things that are alike in some way or are used together 6-7, 8, 9, 11, 13, 15, 18, 22

sorting — putting things that are alike in some way, such as color or size, into groups 4-5, 8, 9, 10, 11, 13, 15, 16, 18, 20, 21, 23

texture — the way something feels, like bumpy tree bark or the smooth skin of an apple 14-15

videos

Bill Cosby's Picture Pages: Shapes and Colors. (Front Row Video)

Math Is Fun series. (Great Plains Instructional Library)

Same and Different. (United Learning, Inc.)

WITHDRAWN